Spot the Differences

Wolf or Coyote?

by Jamie Rice

Bullfrog Books

T0010214

Ideas for Parents and Teachers

Bullfrog Books let children practice reading informational text at the earliest reading levels. Repetition, familiar words, and photo labels support early readers.

Before Reading
- Discuss the cover photo. What does it tell them?
- Look at the picture glossary together. Read and discuss the words.

Read the Book
- "Walk" through the book and look at the photos. Let the child ask questions. Point out the photo labels.
- Read the book to the child, or have him or her read independently.

After Reading
- Prompt the child to think more. Ask: Did you know what wolves and coyotes were before reading this book? What more would you like to learn about them?

Bullfrog Books are published by Jump!
5357 Penn Avenue South
Minneapolis, MN 55419
www.jumplibrary.com

Library of Congress Cataloging-in-Publication Data

Names: Rice, Jamie, author.
Title: Wolf or coyote? / by Jamie Rice.
Description: Bullfrog books.
Minneapolis, MN: Jump!, Inc., [2022]
Series: Spot the differences
Includes index. | Audience: Ages 5–8
Identifiers: LCCN 2021028393 (print)
LCCN 2021028394 (ebook)
ISBN 9781636903552 (hardcover)
ISBN 9781636903569 (paperback)
ISBN 9781636903576 (ebook)
Subjects: LCSH: Gray wolf—Juvenile literature.
Coyote—Juvenile literature.
Classification: LCC QL737.C22 R516 2022 (print)
LCC QL737.C22 (ebook)
DDC 599.773—dc23
LC record available at https://lccn.loc.gov/2021028393
LC ebook record available at https://lccn.loc.gov/2021028394

Editor: Jenna Gleisner
Designer: Michelle Sonnek

Photo Credits: photomaster/Shutterstock, cover (left), 1 (left), 20, 24 (bottom); Jim Cumming/Shutterstock, cover (right), 1 (right), 5, 6–7 (top), 21; Holly Kuchera/Shutterstock, 3, 8–9, 22 (left); Geoffrey Kuchera/Shutterstock, 4; bjmc/iStock, 6–7 (bottom); NaturesDisplay/iStock, 10–11; Cynthia Kidwell/Shutterstock, 12–13, 23tl, 23bl; Karel Bartik/Shutterstock, 14–15, 23tr; Malcolm Schuyl/Alamy, 16–17; Doug Demarest/Design Pics/Getty, 18–19, 23br; Jaymi Heimbuch/Minden Pictures/SuperStock, 22 (right); ilwhaley/iStock, 24 (top).

Printed in the United States of America at Corporate Graphics in North Mankato, Minnesota.

Table of Contents

How to Use This Book

In this book, you will see pictures of both wolves and coyotes. Can you tell which one is in each picture?

Hint: You can find the answers if you flip the book upside down!

Howl and Hunt

This is a wolf.

This is a coyote.

Both look like dogs.

But they are not
the same.

Can you spot
the differences?

fur

A wolf has gray fur.

A coyote's fur can be gray or tan.

Which is this?

Answer: coyote

A wolf's ears are short and round.

A coyote's ears are tall and pointy.

Which is this?

Answer: coyote

snout

Both howl.

A wolf's snout is wide.

A coyote's is narrow.

Which is this?

Wolves hunt in packs.
Coyotes hunt alone.
Which are these?

tail

Both run fast.
A wolf's tail sticks
out when it runs.
A coyote's
hangs down.
Which is this?

Wolves are bigger. Their paws can be as big as your hand.

What do you think left this track?

track

See and Compare

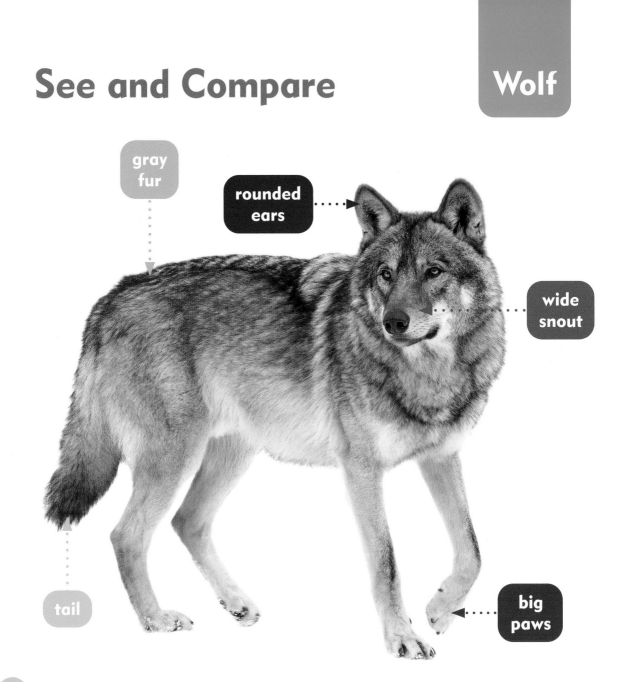

gray fur

rounded ears

wide snout

tail

big paws

20

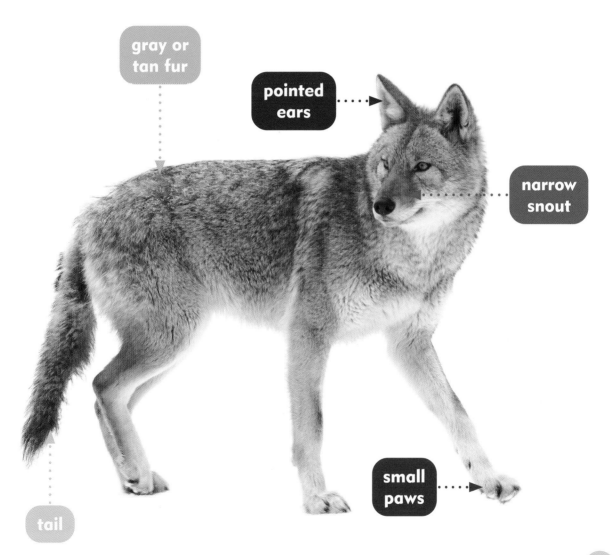

Coyote

gray or tan fur

pointed ears

narrow snout

small paws

tail

21

Quick Facts

Wolves and coyotes are both mammals. They both have fur and give birth to live young. They are similar, but they have differences. Take a look!

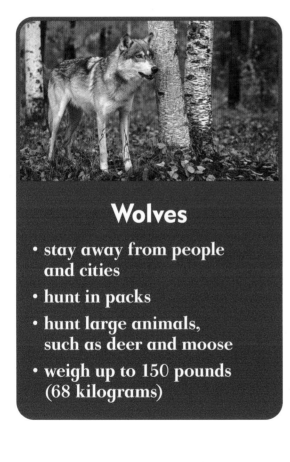

Wolves

- stay away from people and cities
- hunt in packs
- hunt large animals, such as deer and moose
- weigh up to 150 pounds (68 kilograms)

Coyotes

- will live near people and cities
- hunt alone
- hunt small animals, such as rabbits and birds
- weigh up to 50 pounds (23 kilograms)

Picture Glossary

howl
To make a long, loud cry.

packs
Groups of wolves.

snout
The long front part of an animal's head that includes its nose, mouth, and jaws.

track
A mark left by a moving animal.

Index

To Learn More

Finding more information is as easy as 1, 2, 3.

❶ Go to www.factsurfer.com

❷ Enter "wolforcoyote?" into the search box.

❸ Choose your book to see a list of websites.